THOMAS KINKADE

with
Anne Christian Buchanan

Simple Little
Pleasures

Harvest House Publishers

Eugene, Oregon

Simple Little Pleasures

Text Copyright © 2002 Thomas Kinkade, Media Arts Group, Inc.,
Morgan Hill, CA 95037 and Harvest House Publishers, Eugene, OR 97402

Published by Harvest House Publishers
Eugene, OR 97402

Library of Congress Cataloging-in-Publication Data
Kinkade, Thomas, 1958-
     Simple little pleasures / Thomas Kinkade.
        p.cm. – (Simpler times collection)
    ISBN 0-7369-0637-1
   1. Simplicity. I. Title.

   BJ1496 .K56 2002
   179'.9–dc21

                          2001038505

Text for this book has been excerpted from *Simpler Times* by
Thomas Kinkade (Harvest House Publishers, 1996).

Harvest House Publishers has made every effort to trace the ownership of
all poems and quotes. In the event of a question arising from the use of a
poem or quote, we regret any error made and will be pleased to make the
necessary corrections in future editions of this book.

Verses are taken from the Holy Bible, New International Version®.
Copyright © 1973, 1978, 1984 by the International Bible Society.
Used by permission of Zondervan Publishing House.

Design and production by Koechel Peterson & Associates,
Minneapolis, Minnesota

The great doing of little things makes the great life.

—EUGENIA PRICE

When I'm reading our town newspaper, I often browse the want ads. These ads offer a fascinating glimpse into our culture. For example, there seems to be an increasing number of lonely people in the world, because I've noticed more and more ads placed by single people searching for a friend or mate. I've found these ads to be so revealing about people's basic yearnings and needs.

Most of the time, what seems to be missing is romance. People seem especially hungry to take moonlit walks on the beach with a special someone. They yearn for evenings by a fire. They want someone to share music with, special dinners with, unforgettable moments with.

Romance is the glamour which turns the dust of everyday life into a golden haze.

—ELINOR GLYN

Who could blame them? I love those things myself, and I thank God daily I have my lovely wife to share romantic moments with.

But I always find myself wondering about something when I read those "romance wanted" ads. I wonder, do these people ever actually walk on the beach themselves? Do they enjoy fine food and music, savor special moments in their lives, enjoy moonlight and starlight and rainy-day walks beneath an umbrella?

Love doesn't grow on trees like the apples of Eden—it's something you have to make. And you must use your imagination.

—JOYCE CARY

We live in a wonderful world that is full of beauty, charm and adventure.
There is no end to the adventures that we can have if only we seek them with our eyes open.

—JAWAHARLAL NEHRU

Contrary to popular opinion, romance is not a relationship—although it can add fullness and spice and excitement to a connection between two people. Romance is not hearts and flowers and violins, although an evening of hearts and flowers and strings can be soaringly romantic.

Romance is instead an attitude, a set of habits, a way of encountering the world. You are a romantic when savoring experience is a priority for you, when you are willing to invest time and energy into making your experiences more vivid and memorable.

I have long been in the habit of planning special experiences, rewarding myself with simple little pleasures that may cost little but pay high emotional dividends.

For instance, every day I plan my lunch break. I don't just say, "Well, looks like it's noon; better go grab a sandwich or just eat while I work." Instead, I look forward in anticipation to an hour in the fresh air with my lunch in my lap and a book in my hand. Or I make plans to walk to town in the bright spring sunshine, sit on a bench in the square, and watch the people.

That pleasure which is at once the most pure, the most elevating and the most intense, is derived, I maintain, from the contemplation of the beautiful.

—EDGAR ALLAN POE

The other day I decided to spend my lunch break shopping for a small wooden box to give as a gift. I walked downtown and wandered through several antique stores until I found my prize—a wonderful little chest of carved mahogany. Then with my package in hand I meandered down the street to my favorite little café and ordered a cup of coffee.

That was a simple little interlude, and yet it added a special romantic touch to my day. The enjoyment it brought me was far out of proportion to the little energy and money I invested in it.

The life of man is the true romance, which when it is valiantly conduced, will yield the imagination a higher joy than any fiction.

—RALPH WALDO EMERSON

We live in a beautiful world, one that is shimmering with romance. It's all around you, rich and lovely and exciting. It comes into your life when you open yourself to savor your moments—happy and sad, beautiful and mundane, alone or with someone you love.

Of course, there is a special joy in sharing your romantic life with the person you love best in all the world.

My ongoing romance with my wife, Nanette, is one of the constant pleasures of my existence. After many years of marriage, we are countless things to one another—business colleagues, parental partners, and friends.

But we are always and forever lovers, ever seeking out new ways to keep the romantic spark in our life together. We seek out time to be alone together, even if it's just a walk through the neighborhood. We set aside a night each week for a date, dressing up for each other, lighting candles, savoring a kind of quivering formality that reminds us of the times when we were young teenagers falling in love.

Most of all, we plan surprises for each other. We orchestrate special moments, great and small, that show we have listened carefully and observed the other person's wants and needs and invested precious energy just to make each other feel loved. In a sense, the history of our relationship is the history of such planned moments.

I will make you brooches
    and toys for your delight
Of bird-song at morning
    and star-shine at night.
I will make a palace fit
    for you and me
Of green days in forests
    and blue days at sea.
And this shall be for music
    when no one else is near,
The fine song for singing,
    the rare song to hear!
That only I remember,
    that only you admire,
Of the broad road that stretches
    and the roadside fire.

—ROBERT LOUIS STEVENSON

From childhood on I have had the dream of life lived as a sacrament...
The dream implied taking life ritually as something holy.

—BERNARD BERENSON

Nanette savors memories of the anniversary on which I presented her with a framed "early Kinkade." It was a painting of a boy and a girl walking in the moonlight—a portrait of us at a very early point in our relationship. I had painted it years before, after coming home from a date with Nanette, and I had saved it. Now it hangs in a place of honor in our home.

I, in turn, remember the year when Nanette orchestrated a surprise party for my birthday. She went to incredible lengths to prepare the food and put up decorations and sneak thirty of our friends into the house without my suspecting what was going on. And she did it. I was surprised into speechlessness.

Very great achievements are brought about by passion and emotion rather than by practice, training, and knowledge.

—FREDERICK PHILIP GROVE

Such elaborately planned gestures are a treasured element in our romantic life. Some we even plan together, like the trip to Paris we took on our third anniversary. We couldn't afford the trip. We didn't have time to make the trip. But we went anyway, and we had the time of our lives. We came back from that experience with the firelight burning in our hearts.

But romantic moments and gestures need not be so large to be meaningful. Romance can be as simple as a love note hidden in the laundry, a soda with two straws, a shared glance over the heads of the children, a bouquet waiting with a restaurant reservation. It can be an ordinary experience shared—like sports or hiking or sketching. Sometimes, it is the small events that carry the sweetest pleasure and evoke the deepest passion.

In a way, romance is an affirmation and a celebration of the simplest, most important things in life. We romance our lives when we take time to look at each other, to appreciate our experiences and our loved ones, to really live our own lives. Romancing one's life is the most personal of pursuits. It will always reflect the specific interests and talents of the people involved.

You have made known to me the path of life;

you will fill me with joy in your presence;

with eternal pleasures at your right hand.

—PSALM 16:11

When Nanette is sharing her love with me, she usually speaks in her own personal romantic language; she offers me the gift of time and energy. She loves to cook, and she knows I enjoy fine food, so she puts together romantic dinners. She is athletically inclined, and she knows I like to play golf, so she took golf lessons so we could hit the greens together. Because she shares my taste for exploration and adventure, she has strapped on many a backpack and joined me on the trail.

Our moments of inspiration are not lost though we have no particular poem to show for them; for those experiences have left an indelible impression, and we are ever and anon reminded of them.

—HENRY DAVID THOREAU

And of course, I try to employ my own talents to romance my wife. The habit of paying her tribute in my paintings began with a whim and has continued to add a special spark in our life together. Nanette loves it when I hide her initial in my paintings—when I carve "N"s into my painted trees and emblazon them onto the sides of buildings. She loves it when I leave little sketches and silly notes in the house for her. She loves it when I roughhouse with the children and read to them. For her, my involvement in parenting our children is romantic.

Your own romantic language will consist of whatever brings you pleasure, whatever makes you feel alive, whatever makes you feel safe and loved, whatever is most uniquely you. These are the experiences you can savor, the experiences that strengthen your connections to the people you love and to your own heart and soul.

But whether single or married, in love or alone, what does a little romance require but a little planning, a little attention, a little passion?

When it comes to romancing your life, a little goes a long, long way.

They will celebrate your abundant goodness and joyfully sing of your righteousness.

—PSALM 145:7

Life is made up, not of great sacrifices or duties, but of little things, in which smiles and kindness, and small obligations win and preserve the heart.

—HUMPHREY DAVY